Bloom, Roses, Bloom
by Oyedolapo Oyesiji

ISBN: 978-978-984-299-5
ISBN: 978-978-984-300-8 (ebook)

Editors:
Tope Olabisi and Olusade Oyesiji

Cover Design and Book Layout:
Olaoluwa Alabi Studio

Contributors:
Dr. Olabisi Ayodele
Elizabeth Orode
Dolapo Olaleye
Precious Iloloujehme

JANUARY 2023: First Edition

DEDICATION
To the dead, the living and the unborn.

CONTENT

ACKNOWLEDGEMENT

It all started as mere thoughts running through my mind. Then, it became thoughts penned down on the pages of books. Then it became my thoughts in your hand.

While I am grateful to God for the inspiration, I owe an incalculable debt to everyone whose wings I have soared; thank you for believing in me and making me a better person. This project would not exist without you.

I thank my beloved wife and friend - Olusade Oyesiji, for her unflinching support in turning my poems into a book. She is always eager to read, edit and share my works.

I also want to acknowledge the great effort of my editor- Tope Olabisi, whose suggestions, additions and corrections have made this book better. In addition, I appreciate the contributions of Dr. Olabisi Ayodele, Elizabeth Orode, Dolapo Olaleye and Precious Iloloujehme, who, at one time or the other, added to my literary work.

I say thank you to all my family members and friends.

This book is the first of many.

FOREWORD

Through poems, people have found comfort and healing. The culture enwreathing poetry has shaped civilization for thousands of years.

The title of this collection of poems, Bloom, Roses, Bloom, not only fills your heart with hope, it makes you flinch-less, compelling you to sketch out your life according to the will of God.

Meanwhile, despite the abundance of grace, the fragrance of faith, the bloomingness inherent in God, many people have an undercurrent of dread towards life.

Bloom, Roses, Bloom is one of the most irresistibly fascinating books to read in today's unmoored world, where many people have been unboxed, leaving them vulnerable to Satan's thwacking. Put simply, reading this book helps you build aplomb.

The compelling openings, the intriguing rhymes, the exquisite stanzas and the unique verses create empowering feeling in readers.

There is something faith-filled, something intriguing, something blossoming about this collection. It careens you to burgeon.

In this season of life, when the world is fading and is struggling with the loss of normalcy, we need a slew of these - writings about burgeoning.

I have known the author for years. He belongs to a company of people; an ecosystem of writers God has given His Word to publish.

The poems are in various ladders - ladders that are apart yet, overlapping one another. In some places, intertwining their themes to form a narrative. As the reader voyages deeply to them, faith is ignited, then blossoms like an oak in the spring. There is a reclamation, a flourishing happening in the heart, where God takes the centre stage.

The world has withered enough. We need a bloom.

~'Niyi Olamiju
Author, Hormones on Fire & Genes Fall Apart

PROLOGUE

Dear Friend, Hold On.

I know this looks like a carefully
Scripted Hollywood blockbuster
Where the streets are deserted
And all you can hear
Is the howling of winds
Where the dark lantern covers the moon
And memories are in pictures-
Moments captured in time.

I know you miss the crazy city traffic,
The ones that wearied you daily
And the daily bus tales
That sounded like lies.

Just like you my friend
I miss holding the hands
Of my brothers and sisters in prayers,
Lifting holy hands
In the gathering of the saints.

Dear Friend,
Hold on,
These fetters of fear
The shells of pain,
The cloud of loneliness,
Will soon be gone,
And together we will embrace
the fresh rays of the sun
and fresh waves of the sea.

This was written during the COVID-19 pandemic to inspire hope other than fear.

Chapter One
FAITH

The Golden Pen

Covered with cloud of despair
The world sinks deep into depression
Thick fogs block rays of hope
Our misery is f orever stuck with us.

When it rains,
The flood of depression
Fills the room
Seeping through the licking roofs.

When it shines,
We are visited by the scourge of death

Who will tear off this cloud of despair
That covers the heart like stubborn grass in rain?
Who will flip the switch of light,
That darkness has swallowed up in style?

I will write
To paint the picture of Hope
like a skilled painter,
Stroke after stroke
I will paint until the image is clear.

I will write
Not to recount the tales of despair
But to punch holes on this colossal fog
That light might shine and pierce through the despair.

In The Shadows

In the shadows—
Where light barely shines
I saw good and evil
Light and darkness
Our Father must be both,
I thought.

Then, at the appearance of light
All shadows dissipated—gone
Now I know;
Good and evil,
Light and darkness
Can never coexist

I have seen our Father in the light
A beauty to behold
A beauty to know
Always been good
Always been light.

I saw our Father
For who he is
And all variations disappeared.

She Walked on Water

He spoke to her heart
Bypassing her head—
The seat of doubts
He spoke to her heart
Where fear cannot thrive.

Her ears of faith opened
As he sowed seeds in her heart
Like a phoenix she arose
Walking away from the voices of unbelief
that cluttered her head.

She stood,
firmly on word eternal
Faith is here—in her heart
Faith is here—in her mouth
Days of doubts are over
She walked on water.

I Saw the Wind

I saw her
Blow back and forth
She is Lovely to watch,
Not like Hurricane Maria.

I saw her
And ran towards her.
Our hands met
As she dragged me up for a flight

They felt her
But I saw her
I've moved with the wind
And I'm not where I used to be

On the wings of the wind
I soar!

I Want to Live

I want to do beyond surviving,
I want to live;
To glow and replenish;
To blossom like a watered orchard;
To light the world like the daystar;
To spread the rays of hope across
the globe like a sky lantern.

I want to do beyond surviving,
I want to grow in love and grace;
To colour the hearts of men with goodness—
in words and deeds.
I want to rise beyond hatred, pains and hurts;
To build an edifice of love,
in a love-drought world.

I will do beyond surviving,
I will live.

Our Father's Love

We were deep down in a mess
No one could reach out to help
Even the best of us are guilty—
Criminals; death bound.

Our ancestors plagued us
Sentenced us to life imprisonment
And left us without hope
Full of sickness, grief and death.

But love showed up
He took up our hopeless state
And paid the price with his blood—
Unblemished, untainted.

The demands of death He met
He rose, as the first of his kind
He rose, as the life giver.

Condemned by the best of men
Reviled by all he died for
Death, the price paid in hades
Sin, the burden He carried to hell

His life, Essence and Being
His joy, love and strength
He freely gave

This is the Father's love
That divinity will indwell humanity.

The Talebearer Water

I bowed my head in anguish
At the news of the talebearer
His words, cut through like a sword
Left me haemorrhaging in pain.

My blood, boiled with the rage of a bull
I prepared to slay
With words that bite.

A trap it is, now I see
A self-sentence to the prison of offence
I was once freed from
Now I see offence, I run for my life.

Dear offence,
I know you will come sooner or later
But when you come
I would not be tempted to pick you

God Ran.

I pitched my tent against God
I wore my boxing gloves
And challenged Him to fight.
Come out, I said:
Creator of Good and Evil;
Author of Peace and Confusion;
Harbinger of Hope and Hopelessness;
A Saviour and a Destroyer.
Come out, let our fists decide.

God ran towards me, not out of anger
but of love, with an embrace.
All the fury I had in me dissipated.
"I LOVE YOU" was the magic word
That melted my frozen heart.

His words laid eternity bare before me
And made a way for me to see His True Being;
I saw him for who He has always been
A Good God; A Good Father.

God ran to me, not in wrath
but in Love.

Dear Faith

Your words have been my anchor
A rudder, charting my course
A compass, giving direction to my path

You brought your companion,
Patience, to stay with me
As I sail through the turbulent sea of life.
Patience with his heart-warming smile
Amidst heavy storms
Remains unruffled.

Dear Faith
I cannot wait to meet your new friends:
Love, Joy, Peace and Gentleness
As we voyage through
The oceans of life

In victory,
Chanting the triumphant sound,
A song of conquest
In the face of defeat.

Needs and Bills

In a world of needs and bills,
daily remind yourself;
'there's more to live for

In a world of needs and bills,
wear the cloak of selflessness
and rend the veil of selfishness
rooted in greed and materialism.

In a world of needs and bills,
see the earth through the
lens of eternity;
let men through you have
a taste of heaven on earth.

Dear Forgiveness

When I was wrong
You were there all the way
To guide me from getting lost
In the city of self-condemnation
You hosted me in the house of love
And spoiled me with loads of affection

When I was hurt,
you brought healing to do his job
To train my hands
To stitch the wounds of men
And leave the scars
For they tell stories of conquests won.

When I needed help
You became a life line.
Always reminding me—you are here,
to guide you back to the right track".

Dear Forgiveness,
You opened my heart to love and healing
You opened my heart to the beauty of living.

Dear Pain

Dear Pain,
Thanks for the company,
Nothing is wrong with you
But I have met a new friend.

Healing showed me the beauty of pain,
"Stop recounting the tales of woes like a fairy tale," He said.

He stitched my open wound
One thread after the other
I writhed and squeaked.

With a soft kiss on my lips
And a warm smile,
He said:
"I am here to walk you through the Pain,
Until all you know is **Healing.**"

Let There Be Light.

Let there be Light
In the earth, I thought.
But He speaks of my Heart
Where He delights to shine forth.

Father of Light
He chased darkness
Out of my being
Until my heart
Becomes his treasured possession.

I am enraptured by this new reign
Full of life, love and hope
His Spirit within
A surety of His ownership
Of me, His new bride.

Let there be Light
And from within me
He shines forth.
I shine as the bride of Light
I shine as Light.

I laughed at the Devil

When sickness came visiting
It felt as if my body was being dismembered
All I could hear were my organs screeching
This must be world war three.
"My friend, there is no hope,"
Said the doctor.

No Hope, re-echoed the devil
As I watched him laugh,
"You won't survive this
Pack your bags and
Prepare for the journey
To the world beyond,"
He dropped his thoughts full of lies.

So I laughed at the devil and his lies
As I faintly muttered my eternal realities
Till a rush of strength filled my whole being
I shouted at the devil like a wounded lion
I am healed, I am healed!
A coward, he took to his heels
With his hopeless reports.

When sickness came visiting
I laughed at the devil
I laughed at his folly.

I Sat with Wisdom.

I sat with wisdom and
fastened my ears to his words
my heart was his note pad
as he scribbled eternal words on it.

daily he woke me
to instruct me on the path of life
he showed me pitfalls of men
whose greatness were aborted.

he reeled out many who were overtaken
by the strong waves of the sea
for they despised instructions
that would have made them surf above the winds.

I sat with wisdom
and he engraved his words in my heart
as I sail through the sea of life
his words became my rudder.

Treasure.

Treasure
wandered off the path of value
fraternized with the swine.

The pigs—
used to dirt—
Discerned her as a toy
In turn, they rubbed her with dirt
Until every sense of worth is gone.

Let treasure know,
That value is based on recognition
Let treasure know,
That a companion of the Swine
will feast on dirt

Let treasure know,
That the Swine wasn't designed
to honour value.

I am More

He is a whale,
Big enough for the Ocean
But nothing more.

He is a storm,
The type that only moves trees
But not strong enough
to pull down rocks and strong mountains

He smiled,
stood and defined himself:

I am more than Ocean
What I am licks up the great seas.
I am more than the Storm
What I am pockets Tsunamis.
I am more than fire
I am what fire sees and takes to flight.

I am the extension of divinity in humanity
I am immortality in mortality.

Just like a Child

When I was a child
the world was a canvas where—
I painted beautiful
pictures of impossible imagery.

until the voice of the child in me was
muffled by husky-adults;
Who bullied me into believing that
my imaginations were devoid of reality.

Little did they know
That dreams and reality are siblings
Who need each other to survive
Not enemies

I broke free, from the prison of adulthood
Which muffled the voice of the child in me
And veiled my imaginations with pessimism.

Just like a child,
I set out to take the world;
Without inhibitions.

The Beloved of the Father

I don't want to be a star
For I can't outshine them
In the galaxy.
I don't want to be a sun
With brightness that blinds
I don't want to be a moon,
That lights up the night
I don't want to be an angel
With fiery eyes and looks.

I am okay being a New Man
The essence of creation
The apex of God's workmanship
The habitation of the Father.

I am okay being Me,
The beloved of the Father.

Abba Father

Abba Father,
Many have accused you of being bipolar—
Good and evil emanates from you, they claim
But I see you clearly in the face of Jesus
You are Good
You are Light
You are God.

How We Live

You've heard life is hard
Difficult and terrible
You wake up daily preparing
for the worst.

They've killed the beauty of living
And snuffed out from you
The essence of your existence.

We are of faith
Our expectations, ambitions,
Aspirations and words
Are those of faith.

That's how we live
That's how to live.

Let it Burn

Let it burn, Let it burn
Let it burn the souls of men
Let it burn out the chaffs that have
veiled their eyes.

Let it burn, let it burn
Let it lick off the blood of death
That life may flow ceaselessly
through their veins.
Let it burn out the rage of hell
And the fear that has imprisoned
their souls.

Let the fire of your love burn
And consume Nations.

Origin

I hail from the thought of divinity
long before the cosmos had its identity
I was formed in the clay of love
to be an enigma for all other forces of the earth.

I hail from where there is no light or darkness
Where the Sun never rises and the Moon never sets
I hail from where the reflection of the Father
is enough to be our light.

I hail from where precious stones
difficult to describe are
where angels were made to serve Man
the only true being that delights the creator.

I hail from Zion
now seated at the right hand
where I ought to be
as it was in the beginning
in the thought of Divinity.

This is my Root;
This is my History;
This is my Origin.

Oceans Can Be Conquered

I stood still at the shore of the ocean
With the desire to conquer it
Just like I conquered the rivers and the seas
There the wind howled
And doubts whispered into my ears:
Oceans can't be conquered.

For once I was terrified
Of the endless width of the ocean
The depths unexplored and
The ravenous whales and sharks
waiting to feast on the misguided dreamer
who wants to conquer the ocean.

Leave the shore and set for sail
The ocean is more terrified of you
Than you are of it
Leave the shore and set for sail
Oceans can be conquered
Faith roars from within.

Listen

Listen,
The storm is too small
To pull us down
The sea is too small
To drown us.

Listen,
Our footing is stronger
Than that of the rock
Our strength is more
Than a million rhinoceros

Listen
Fear is too weak
To hold us back
No wall is too tall
To keep aground.

Listen,
There is an endless supply
Of strength that booms from within
There is abundance to feast on.

Listen,
The Lord is within
The King is here.

The god that begs.

Have you seen the god that begs?
the god of the belly
that takes from the poor
to enrich the rich.

have you seen the god that begs?
who gives breath free of charge
but provision is made by barter.

have you seen the god that begs?
the one who only speaks
through a priest
that can never be questioned.

have you seen the god that begs?
he is in the belly of man
who is consumed with greed
this is not the God that dwells
in the heavenlies.

The Spirit of Faith

I won't walk through life
Full of fear fueled by doubts
The uncertainties echoed
By men whose hearts have surrendered
To the battering of life.

I won't walk through life
With my head bowed in defeat
Full of thoughts of what should have been
And what could have been.

I have an anchor, a sure guide
I have a compass, true and through
I have a sure word, the Holy writing
Inspired of God, penned by men
I have my faith, grounded
on this unfailing words.

I won't walk through life
In defeat and fear
I have the Spirit of Christ
The Spirit of Faith.

The Rest of my Days

The rest of my days
In strength I live
Just like wine
I get better with time
The rest of my days
Is the best of my life

The rest of my days
In wisdom I rule
Discerning always the truth—
The words of men
To the bones and marrow
Those who mortgage the living truth
For a loaf of mortal bread
The rest of my days
Is the best of my life.

The rest of my days
In consecration with sacrifice
With sincerity of heart
I stay true to the cause of the Lord
Beyond fads and trends
And the changing words of men
The rest of my days
Is the best of my life.

Don't Look Back

Don't look back
Your hands have ploughed hectares of land
Your seeds have grown into a fruitful vineyard

Don't look back
Listen not to the voices of pride
That have taken many down
To the pit deeper than hell

Don't look back
To watch the ways of darkness
You were once stripped of
The lies that sound like truth
The brass that shines like gold.

Don't look back
The plough is still in your hands
There is a God waiting ahead
To reward greatly
Your sacrifice in Obedience
Don't look back.

As I Rise

Daily as I rise
Before the rising of the Sun
Don't let me be lost
In the hustle for survival
And forget the love that found me in death.

Daily as my needs increase
Don't let me be lost
In the pursuit of things
That I miss your words
The ones that daily shaped my day
Before I became too busy to listen.

Daily as I work
Towards my dreams
Don't let me be lost in the crowd of men
That live without a cause
Don't let your voice now sound
Like echoes to my ears.

Be Strong, Be Unmovable.

Be strong, be unmovable
The way the mountain stays strong
Through the frosty winter and the hot summer
Through the cyclones and the uproar of great seas.

Be strong, be unmovable
Like the Iroko tree
Whose roots are locked
In the hearts of the rocks
Who stands tall
When other trees
Bow to the tune of the windstorms.

Be strong, be unmovable
Like a soldier on duty
Weathers hunger and thirst.
Brave out drought and famine
Until abundance rains like ice crystals
Be strong, be unmovable.

Father of Light

Father of light
Shinned in my heart
Like in the beginning
Before the earth was conceived.

Father of Love
Faithful and true
Poured his life for me
Even when in unbelief I chose death.

Father of Light
Through faith in his words
He quickened me
And death fled like bees
With faith in my heart
Unbelief was crushed
Never to rise again.

Father of Light
Fulfilled all his promises
In the gift of his Son
In the gift of Himself.
Salvation demystified
In the saving hands
of the Father of Light.

Man in Christ

I am a Man in Christ,
A fountain of wisdom hewn in God
A shining light whose brightness is God
I am precious and beautiful.

I am a Man in Christ,
A light whose shinning fills the earth
A partaker of life divine
A beauty to behold.

I am a Man in Christ,
Extension of divine love to men
Recipient of Love Unconditional
Minister of reconciliation.

I am a Man in Christ,
Son of light and revelation
Habitation of the Father

Arike.

Arike,
Your smile strikes the lightning of hope
Breaking through the doubts of my heart
Your words, like honeycomb
Melt with sweetness
From the depths of my heart
To the core of my bones.

You picked up the pieces of my heart
And fixed it like a skilled craftsman.
You built an edifice from the ruins of my past
And turned my scars into a great piece of art.

The angels peep down
Just to have a glimpse of your beauty
Mortals stand stupefied
at your unwonted graciousness
She must be a goddess, they claim.

Arike,
You're more than a goddess
You're the Queen of my Heart
My seat of intelligence
The Khalesi of my Kingdom
The definition of a Masterpiece.

Arike: A Yoruba name.
Khalesi: A character in the game of thrones.

If Our Love Could Be Forever.

If our love could be forever
I would make a request in heaven
to walk with you on the streets of gold
Watching the angels sing
And stand envious of our love story.

If our love could be forever
I would ask for you to sit
on the throne made with gold
That I may renew my vows
made to you on earth.

But such love doesn't exist in heaven
So let me pour out my heart
Now to you, my Love
Before we get to the world beyond
Where we will just be friends.

Where is my Love.

You set the fire of love
Burning fiercely in my heart
Till it burnt my soul
Your demeanour was not of a deceiver
So I recklessly left my heart in your care

I woke up and you were gone,
I searched for you
On the hills of love,
Passed through the wilderness of lust
Walked straight to the valleys of deceit
Looking for you, my lover

Hoping you had missed the route
that leads straight to my heart.
If I find you, I can show you the path
You once walked.

My love, the lover
You taught me how to start this flame of love
Not how to quench it.
Now I have burnt cities,
Save me from burning the world.

Where is my love?
Where is my lover?

Dear Heart (Co-written, Dr. Ayodele)

Dear Heart,
Don't just pump blood,
Find Love
Give Love
Receive Love.

Fall in Love
Stand in Love
Laugh in Love
Choose to Love
Find the Queen—
worthy of Your crown

Keep love; firmly retain
No love from you must roam;
Desertion isn't attraction;
Only in love do hearts rest

Don't just pump blood
Find Love.

Tourist

She treated his heart like a part-time gig
Freelanced with his emotions.
He shut the door to his heart;
Vacation is over
The tourist heads back home.

Love Story

The best of love stories have been written
The best of love songs have been sung
But yours is what I choose to daily listen to
From now, till my hair turns grey.

You will always remain the treasure
I keep in my heart
Where no one else can reach.

Our Creed

Take my hands as I take yours
On our knees, we forge this union
before the Father of Light
Together, we will withstand storms
life throws at us
We will conquer territories
with our Faith in Him

We will chase out darkness
in the heart of men
With our mouth
we will speak forth light
Our home will be a safe Haven
for men destitute of God

Our model is Christ:
In Love and Forgiveness
In Conduct and Words
In Faith and Hope
In Life and Death.

Till we see the Father,
In Life or Death.

Àkànbí

Àkànbí,
You're a soldier
You're my warrior
Warriors don't sheath their swords
In the heat of the battle
So be strong,

I know you feel
this is the breaking point
and failure is imminent
Àkànbí, you've conquered nations
Conquer this fear also

Rise up,
sharpen your swords
and pick up your shield
You're the master of war
Posterity will always remember.

Àkànbí, okùnrin ogun,
Gbéra nle.

Àríké.

Akanbi: an indigenous Yoruba name.
Okunrin Ogun: Man, of war.
Gbera nle: Rise up

My Love to You (conversations)

Anike,

I accept the totality
of your being:
Your body, soul and spirit.
I accept your flaws,
but choose to fix my gaze
on your growth process.

I love your scars and the
stories behind them
Anike, even in imperfections,
you are the signature of flawless beauty.

This is my Love to You.

Àkànbí.

Akanbi and Anike are Yoruba indigenous name.

Yoruba Demons

He slid into my DM
Left me mesmerized
As his words took away my senses.
He skilfully unlocked
the bolt of my heart
hooking me at my weakest.

Just like his cohorts,
the demons in him
have blinded him
from seeing
the one that truly
loves him.

That's typical of
Yoruba Demons.

Yoruba Demons: A word used to describe Casanovas.

Hello Love.

Hello Love,
I heard when you are around
I will have butterflies
Flying in my Heart
And I will smile sheepishly
At jokes dry as dust.

I heard when you are around,
Hours is not enough
To behold the gaze of my lover
And to fellowship with beauty of her words.

Am I an exception to this love story?
It seems as if my butterfly is dead.

Love, when next you come
Come with wild butterflies
Let me have a feel
Of what the world speaks of.

Home

It was a long drive
away from home
Into the wild,
Where love only exists in the mind.

Like a skilled stone carver
You carved a cave in your heart
Where I can call home
Far from the predators in the wild
Waiting to feast on my heart.

Now, when I think of home,
All I see is You.

Heart of Gold

Her heart is of gold
More precious than expensive artefacts
So he went digging into mines
Hoping he would find her heart
buried in the belly of the soil.

Her heart is of gold
Not the type buried beneath
the depth of the soil
But the one divinity can attest to.

Her heart is of gold
The man who houses this treasure
In an earthen vessel
Owns a Priceless inheritance.

His Wish

He only wished
Her words were as pretty as
her looks
But her heart stinks more
than a septic tank of a thousand depth.

Love and Porsche

My Love and Porsche,
This our Love can Pause
Because your love for Porsche
Is affecting my Pulse.

Orente won't complain, I thought
because she doesn't want Ferrari.
Now I need an assurance
That true Love is not about Porsche.

Pause, says my Purse,
If your Love is Porsche
Please take a walk
With your Porsche-Love.

———————————

Orente: Beautiful girl.

The Favourite Part of my Song.

You are the favourite part of my song,
The one I always sing even in my dreams;
You're the chorus that stays on my mind,
When the verses are slipping away.

You are the favourite part of my song,
The part that brings out the dancer in me;
You're my perfect harmony;
With incredible symphony.

You are the favourite part of my song,
The chords that send sensation to my spine;
You are the smooth riffs and runs
that make my heart skip;
You are the music I always put on repeat.

Love at First Sight.

Don't love me at first sight,
That's the bright side
Love me when the light is off,
Where all you see is my dark side.

Don't love me when the music is loud,
And the crowd is cheering me on
Love me when the music is off,
and the crowd is gone;
Though I paid my dues.

Don't love me at first sight,
That's the bright side;
Love me beyond the fantasies
scripted in the seat of your mind.

Don't love me at first sight,
That's easy to do
Love me because you know
love is beyond emotions.

Asake

Akanji,
Listen to these words of wisdom:
There are wounds sorry cannot heal
Don't break Asake's heart
before you realize that.

Asake gave you her heart
As a seal of her love
Guard it well
Therein lies true beauty
When shapes and curves are gone.

Abeje

Abeje,
You ran to me to find solace
From the lascivious eyes of men
In your mind, I am a superman
And in the confines of my kingdom
You felt safe
Frolicking in ways unimaginable

I wish you knew the battles fought
To stay sane in a lust driven cosmos
Where words have lost their true meanings:
One corner—a sexual stimulant.

So that I don't fail you
As the hero preconceived
In the depth of your jejune mind
Be guided,
There is a war and the mind
Is the battle ground
This temptation is real

Heart *(co-written, Dolapo Olaleye)*

You care too much, it is smothering.
You call too often, it is riling.
Don't get me wrong,
You did nothing wrong
I simply don't know
how it feels to feel
Your heart is never the problem
It is the lack of mine.

I want to be your cardiologist
Fixing your broken heart
I want to unfreeze your heart
Till love pours out
Like a fresh morning dew
Glowing like the morning sun
Until you know how it feels
To Love again.

Ajoke Ade

Ajoke Ade
If the beautiful ones are yet to be born
I wonder what they will look like
Your kind of beauty
Even the gods envy
You are a foretaste of an immortal beauty
In a mortal body.

Heart Rumblings

Can you hear the rumblings?
Like the sound of war
Listen patiently
To those thuds
She is trying to muffle
Listen patiently to her heartbeats
Hear the words unspoken
If you listen carefully
You won't be deceived
By her calm demeanor
Can you hear the rumblings of her heart?

Aduke.

Aduke mi,
In a busy noisy world
You heard my heart
Calling for acceptance
You drew closer
Dressed in compassion
With reassuring words, you said:
Adigun mi,
Find acceptance from within
What you yearn for
Is already within reach.

---

mi means mine

Fast and Furious

Thinking you will drive with care
I gave you the keys to my heart
Never knew you do racing
The "fast and furious" type.
You took the journey
From my heart to my thighs
Leaving the virgin land bankrupt
Now I will wait for the one that deserves it.

Bruised Heart

A peep through the door of his heart
And all I saw were wounds
There must have been a war
His heart must have been the battlefield
Little wonder he is cold
With periodic sighs and sobs

Baby, I am not a surgeon
But bring me into the core of your heart
Let me watch you heal
If that is all I can do
To make the pains go away.

Assurance

This melody of Love
That plays in our hearts
Has fueled our bond
A fire that forged our hearts
Together as one.

This tune of Love
Like a wing, has carried us
Through the dark and gloomy days
That ought to sniff life out
Of the flame of our love.

This beat of love
Has given us strength
To dance through
The quirks and scorns of men
That kill the pureness of Love.

Let this sound of Love
Now take us to the city
Where fear cannot thrive
Let it birth assurance
Stronger than a thousand Stallions.

Anike

Àníké,
My prized possession.
The jewel that is kept safe
In the depth of my heart.

Àníké,
The beauty that shines brighter
Than ten suns put together
The Queen that glows
Than the biggest of stars

Àníké,
Ìbàdí àrán covered with precious cowries
My wonder of the dawning day
And the Queen of bejeweled night
The one whose mind
Eledua has illuminated

Àníké
The young beauty that speaks
the wisdom of ages to come.

Anike- A Yoruba name
Ibadi aran- buttocks of velvet
Eledua- God

Love Again

hey,
you've opened your heart to vandals
who saw your treasure chest
as a get-rich-scheme
and looted the vault of your heart
of its precious gems.

Now,
the gate of your heart
is filled with an array of army
enough to win the world war.

hey,
don't shut the gate of
the palace of your heart
and the deprive the inhabitants
of your love.
don't imprison your love
in the cocoon of your heart.

hey,
love again.

Chapter Three

LIFE

Hey Rejection

Hey rejection,
Long before I tried
I knew one day you would come
With your foul words
Just to weaken my grit.

Hey Rejection,
Fear has delivered your mail
That I failed again
At proving to men
That I am a hub of ingenuity.

But you need to know that
I have my heart shielded
From your poisoned arrows
That could leave me paralyzed
From trying again.

Hey Rejection,
Even if you've won a hundred times
I am not the type that cowers in defeat.

When I am gone.

Don't come to my grave
When I am gone to the world beyond
To sing encomiums
I was ignorant of
When I had breath
Basking in my lungs

Don't immortalize me with words
When death has touched my soul
And I am six feet
In the depths of earth

Now that I am alive,
Pour out your heart to me
Let me revel in the memories
Of your words

For the dead is deaf
To the eulogies of the living

Kill the Fear

For the fear of being wrong
I shut my voice
Killed my identity
Lurked around in the shadows of myself

Will I be heard?
Will my voice really matter?
Do I have the wits?
I questioned my identity

I hinged on the opinion of men
For self-approval and self-worth
Forgot that approval or disapproval
Does not change who I am

A coward, wallowed in self-pity

With no spine of conviction
Yet sat on the mine of untapped ingenuity
Rejected the beauty of my true-self
In awe of another's
Now I know that until I embrace the core of my being
Men's thousand hugs won't give me warmth.

Will I hide behind the curtains of cowardice?
Will I muffle the strength of my inner being?
No! I will rise and speak from the profundity of my convictions
I will speak and watch fear take flight, never to return

Dear Fear.

Dear Fear,
You delight in hiding in the shadows;
Mystifying the unknown
Making the beats of failure
For all to dance
You mask under the guise of 'comfort zone'
To evade the consequences of change

You, witty-old King of illusions,
Hypnotizing the minds of men;
With words of doubts and impossibilities
Your trump card, failure
Made men bow to your wits.
"All hail the King," "Long live the King."

Your lullabies have laid to sleep
Dreamers and their incredible dreams
Turned potential world changers
Into scramblers for survival
Murdered their ingenuity,
Imprisoned their creativity

If they only knew,
You were a king of illusions
They won't be bound by your imaginary prison.

Pick your Battles

He was pushed and pinned against the wall
Incited with tirade of words
Geared towards hatred and malice
They waited for him to start a war.

But he was wise
He intelligently picked his battles
He broke the wall
Ran for his life

When next you are pushed against the wall
Pause to know
When to start a war
And when to take a walk

Not all battles are meant to be fought.

Break Free

Son,
Like a trash in the bin
You were treated
Like a shit in the hole
You were named

Everyone called you an outcast
Treated you like a Curse
'Cos of your flaws

Stand up Son,
From the bed of misery and self-pity
Break the claws
Men have held you with.

Break Free.

Dad.

Dream Big

Dream big
far beyond the cosmos
Such that scares heaven into you
Keeping you awake all night
Working off your lazy bones

Big dreams are fickle fantasies
When hard work is wanton.
Hard work, a lazy man's curse
Hard work, the meal of the diligent.

The World and Words

The world and words:
pain and hurts
love and kindness
All seen in words.

The world and words:
joy and happiness
hatred and grief
All shown in words.

The world and words:
The social divide;
Rich and poor
Defined in words

The world and words:
ugly and beautiful
The white or black
named in words.

The world, full of men
Men, full of words
poisoned the world.
Men full of words
Beautify the world.

A Fool

I saw a fool
Who stoned his Father
with words
At the market square.

The tale of his
Father's nakedness
Was his favourite song
He sang to his friends

His friends laughed and mocked
His Father disdainfully
At the pub,
Where bottles were buried

I wish he knew
That the child who calls
His Father a Devil
must himself be a demon.

Without A Sliver Spoon

I didn't know what a
silver spoon looked like
I didn't have to
I was in love with the plastic spoon
my parents offered—
It was all they had.

But they offered more
Than a plastic spoon
With their rare heart of gold
I was forged
In contentment
I was raised

I was taught how to fly—
For lack of a sliver spoon
Was not lack of wings
I was taught how to run
Not competing with men
But with self

I was taught
to be without a sliver spoon
Was not a death sentence.

Shadow Chasers

You worked hard,
night and day
just to prove a point
to men with insatiable desires
and hare-brained expectations.

with the momentary applause
they moved on
you are no more trending
so you worked harder
repeating the vicious cycle
until you drove yourself nut.

the ones you set out to impress
didn't even see the point
they left you lonely
on the path of
shadow chasers.

Will you be my friend?

Will you be my friend
When the whole world turns its back?
Will you still be there
When I need a shoulder to lean on?

The loads might not get lighter
But the shoulders must get broader
And the burden becomes easier
When shared on loyal shoulders

I will be there,
Through thick and thin
I will cover you
when you're stripped off your clothes
for I know what it means
to be out alone in the cold

True friendship is hard they say,
Because it starts from the heart.

Hey Offence.

Hey offence,
Come and pick your baggage
you left the last time you checked in.

I once entertained you, not knowing
You are full of mischief
Your words are poisonous
Laced with bitterness and hatred.

Your heart only knows pain
and forgiveness is alien to you.
Come and pick your baggage
I am done entertaining you.

Not a Fool

She cursed her mum
But promised to bless mine
I smiled,
I wasn't raised a fool.

She loathes her mum
But promised to praise mine
I laughed,
I wasn't raised a fool

Let me fly.

Why you wanna fly?
I raised you amongst hens
And hens don't fly

Why you wanna fly?
The ground is big enough
For you to walk and live
What's up there that is not
Right here on the ground?

Let me fly, Let me fly
I was born for flight
To touch the clouds
Kiss the moon and
Smile at the Sun.

Let me fly, Let me fly
Let me play with the stars
Let me soar up to the hills
And build my nest
Where hens can only imagine

Let me fly, Let me fly.
I fly, I fly.

Inspired by Nina Simeone's Blackbird.

Amebo.

Aduke,
I heard at the village square
Adio took to his heels
because Amope took a knee
With a ring in her hand.
Hmm, Adio- the trickster.

I also saw a group of young boys
At Ojaoba, queuing to buy "baby Kingsway"
Oh, I mean "sex dolls", with their life savings
What will an adult be doing with sex dolls?
My curiosity will not kill me.

Aduke, aye ti baje o
Young men are now lost in lust
Walking down the path of doom with glee,
Lust has opened the coffins where they will lie,
After mating with their dolls.

Aduke mi, whilst Adio took to his heels,
I am ready to take both knees
And put a ring on it, though I'm not Lord of the Rings
While others replace their Opeke with Dolls,
Take the key to the door of my Heart.

Amebo: Gossips.
Ojaoba: King's Market.
Aye ti baje: The world is corrupt.
Opeke: Beautiful girl.

Take time to grow

Take time to grow
Take time to learn
Learn in quietness
The storm will howl
The wind will blow
As long as the tree
Is deeply rooted
It will dance to the
howling of the wind
That ought to destroy it.

Learner

Every pro was a learner
who confronted their fears
and took the first steps
in the journey of life
to break free from the prison of fear.

with wobbling feet;
quivering hands,
nervous voice,
they set out to take the world.

like a skilled boxer in the ring;
they threw each jab to weaken the
the grip of fear
that has held them spellbound.

fear, a coward;
ran at the tenacity of the determined mind
with persistent and consistent actions
taken in little steps.

every pro was once a learner;
that never succumbed to the word "I can't".

Slavery.

trap; trapped,
don't think: this is what to think.
be blind to the truth;
be deaf to the cry of your heart
trap; trapped.

trap; trapped,
your voice will unnerve the King
for the voice of truth
is a sound of war
in a kingdom built on falsehood.

trap; trapped,
what do you do
when you dine with the King,
who sits on the throne of deception?
Guillotine awaits,
the one who questions the King.

trap; trapped,
pick up the cloak of sycophancy
and cover the vestures of truth.
dine with the King; enslave your tongue.
A night with the King; the beginning of slavery.

Pawn

Push him to the battlefield
where the heat of fire is
The Queen must live.

Thousands of pawns
have been sacrificed
But for the ego of the King
A thousand more must die
For the Queen to live.

Pawns
Have no chance to choose
Which battle they fight

They only pray
That the King they serve
Will not use them
As a tool to service his ego.

Take me to the workshop

Don't just bring me to the showroom
Leaving me awestruck
Of the beauty of your masterpiece
Take me to the workshop
That birthed the showroom.

Make me see the candles you burnt
Throughout the sleepless nights
And bridges you crossed
Just to keep the bird of your dream
Flying

Make me see the times when
you went on recess
Shedding off wings of discouragement
Just for freshness to breathe again
On your dream.

Take me down to the workshop
Where hands get dirty
And creativity is forged in consistency.

Fertile Man.

He is fertile,
He spreads his seeds
across the soil of several wombs
and his fruits filled the earth.

He is fertile,
to populate the earth
but not to care for
the products of his seeds.

He is fertile,
He raised whirlwinds
walking on two legs.

He is fertile,
to start windstorms
others must tame.

Prison.

She is the ice
He is the volcano.
When he erupts
She calms his fury

But at his highest
boiling point
His Lava swallowed
off the Ice.

She is still the ice
Screaming out of the magma
Where her gentle
soul is imprisoned.

She was the Ice
Lost in the lava of his rage;
A gentle soul
with fiery eyes.

Farabalè! (Calm down!)

Can you make the sun come out before its time?
Can you make the moon shine at noon?
Can you turn the day into night?
Can you turn winter into summer?
Farabalè!

Can a tree grow overnight?
Can a foetus mature into a baby in a day?
Can a city be built in a day?
Can love be built in a day?
Farabalè!

Life is a combination of Time and Process,
Growth works with Time and Process;
Time and Process work with Patience;
Farabalè!

Let the day run its course;
Let the night exude its beauty;
Let them meet your hands diligent;
And your heart grateful.

Keep the dreams alive;
Let Hope saturate your being;
And let Patience have its full course.
In all that you do,
Farabalè!

Oreke, The Slay Queen

Oreke, the slay Queen
The radiance of your beauty fills the room
With fragrance irresistible
Your words, just like bees
Sting with pain indescribable.

Nobel men,
Far and near,
Had come bearing gifts
Awestricken by your beauty.
A month with you was worse
Than an excursion in hell.

Oreke,
Grace is the true sexiness
The type real men crave for
That my dear,
Is the definition of a slay queen.

The Tester

Not all waters can be tested
Some rivers have the depths of an ocean
Only few lucky ones
Come back alive.

Not all waters can be tested
Even the skilled swimmers have drowned
In the rivers they thought
Were too shallow.

Not all waters can be tested
For the monstrous beasts of the seas
Await to prey on the
Foolish adventurer.

One Day

One day you will be
where you desired to be
Before you get there, ensure you
Find peace
Find Love
Find Fulfillment and Joy.
Peace, Love, Fulfilment and Joy
Are not location bound
They flow from within.

Embrace Freedom

Uncle No, Uncle Why?
Was all Amope could say
Her innocence destroyed
Opening her into a new world
She was never prepared for.

Amope, writhing and quivering in pain
Of the reality of her new world
Disdainfully starred at her Uncle
Who sat reminiscing in regret.
Ha! Aunty Oreke ti paa mi
Abused turned abuser
He muttered to himself.

I bent a knee, held her hands
Looked into her broken soul
From the gate of her eyes and said:
Amope, forgive and heal
Break this cycle
Of the abused turned abuser
Embrace freedom.

––––––––––––––––––––––––

Amope: A Yoruba name.
Ti paa mi: Have killed me

Why *(Co-written- Elizabeth Orode)*

Their hearts burnt with wrath
And their thoughts went wild with envy
Yet I called them friends
I climbed Mount Everest
They cheered me with words
But pushed me off the cliff
In their thoughts
They were blind to their strength
But envious of mine
Why?

A thousand birds can dance to the winds
Coloring the sky
With their beautifully arrayed wings
They spread around the globe as they fly.
Why cut off my wings
When you can fly
Why stop my flight
When your wings are not fractured
Why push me off the cliff
When we can both fly across the world.

Shine On

Shine on,
More than the brightest stars
Let the sun adore your brightness
And let the moon kiss
the feet of your rising.

Make the earth your canvas
Colour it with beauty
Just like the rainbow
beautifies the cloud.

Blossom;
Spread your roots
across the earth
Let your branches be fruitful
Let them feed the sons of men.

Let your fountain be of endless wisdom
That ceaselessly flows
From depths eternal.
Let men drink from the spring
That flows from your being.

Shine on.

I saw the signs

I saw the signs,
Scattered around the sky:
Of sun turning blue-blood;
And moon turning black;
But I am no astrologist,
So I only wondered what they were.

I saw the signs
Of incessant snaps and fiery eyes;
Anytime an argument ensued,
But I am no psychologist,
So I wondered what they meant.

I saw the signs,
Of body shaking and objects flying
When anger sets in.
Maybe that's who he is;
Maybe he meant no harm;
I must be belaboring on nothing.

Now I understand the signs,
Watching him always
lay his hands on me;
Serving me slaps as daily bread;
Putting in focus the blurry signs.

I can now see the signs,
So clear like a crystal ball;
With black eyes, swollen lips,
swollen cheeks and broken heart—
My new signature.

You are not Alone

You are not alone
Our roots may differ
our background dissimilar
our story definitely unidentical
and our journey diverse.

But we are one in desire
moving up and fighting against the tides
ignoring the odds and pushing still
holding on to strength when we seem weak
believing in the living reality of our dreams
daily pushing, believing, and working hard
until our story reads: against all odds.

to all with a dream bigger than them
You are not alone.

Gossips

They poured the fuel
Romped, frolicked carelessly with fire
Like a fluffy teddy bear
But stunned
When the houses
Danced ballet
To the beats of the flames.

The fuel of gossips
Starts as a little tittle-tattle
But like a wildfire
It spreads like a firestorm.

Evolution *(Co-written Ilolo-Ose)*

The constant hope for today
As has been the obsession of
My thoughts since yesterday
Has kept my heart vigorously
Pumped with blood and
my blood furiously flowing with passion.
My evolvement has meant passing on the torch,
Not from the "young to old" or "old to aged"
But from fear to courage
Freedom to dream some more
Freedom to live, not just exist
I am an example of Evolution
I am the picture of Freedom.

To the dreams of yesterday
A figment of my imagination
That stands now as a reality
Central to my existence
I evolved.
From the fears of the future
That eroded with the winds of growth and change
I evolved.
From the fears of today
To the dreams of the future
The passion that beats in the core of my being
I am evolving.
Yanking off the chains of fear
Breathing the breath of freedom
I am evolving
As a freeman
As a man of Faith.

Kingdom

A kingdom built on lies
Will crumble like a pack of cards
At the sight of truth.

A life built on falsehood
Is like a city ravished by war
It remains desolate.

Little Things

The little things matter—
Others will shove them aside—
But embrace them
Hold them dearly
Even in big moments
The little things always matter.

Letter to My Daughter

Baby Girl,
Learn keenly
overtly and covertly,
let your days get better
just like wine tastes better
with time.

write deeply
bring from the depth of your being
words that transcend time
you are a stream of inspiration,
whose source is endless.

speak
be the voice of those
whose voices have been stifled
by fear and timidity.
speak, without the fear of being wrong.

forgive
the bond of life is tied with
the twine of forgiveness
your heart must be knit
with the thread of mercy
and your mouth full of compassion.

Love
Let this be the building block
your being is founded on
for nothing is as strong as the
force that love emits.

Be sincere
to admit when you are wrong
Be bold
for courage is not gender sensitive.

Baby girl,
In all that you do,
be humane.

They Tried

They kept drowning us in the sea of hatred
But like Dolphins
we turned the depth into a playground.

They kept throwing us off the cliff
But like Eagles
Height helped our flight.

They kept burying us in the ground
But like seeds,
we sprout into a forest
too thick to destroy.

They tried burning us to the ground
But like Gold
The furnace refined us.

While You Wait.

while you wait
for the big things you desire
let your hands get busy
with the little things
that surround you.

while you wait
for that time
when your hands will bless
thousands of lives
start with the twos and threes
and the few around you.

while you wait,
for the world to get better
before the streams of goodness
flow through you
let the world meet you
making it habitable.

while you wait,
for the things you desire
let your hands get busy.

Why Give Up

why give up?
that is easy
try something new
persevere.

why quit?
that is easy,
do something brave,
work harder.

why quit?
that is easy,
history is for
those who stayed through
history is for those who
never quit.

Life is Better

Life is better
When you lay to rest
The beast of bitterness
and embrace the beauty in forgiveness

Don't be deceived
Bitterness eats up more than cancer
Leaving your whole being
At the mercy of anger.

Life is better
When your choice is forgiveness
It is like a breaking of a new day
It fills your soul with freshness.

When we let go
Of hurts and pains.
and hold on tightly
to the peace in forgiveness,
Life is better.

Grief.

a million words
playing in the field
of the mind
all expressed in
unceasing flow of tears
with deep sighs.

the memories
vividly playing out
of words unsaid
and love unexpressed.

can time please be kind
to take me back
to those moments
where I can make amends.

the pain in grief
is not in the gravity of loss
it is the loss of uncaptured moments
and unvoiced love.

Be careful

Be careful
Of the advice of men
Who feed on mischief
As a daily course.

Be careful of men
With self-acclaimed titles
Of kings of orderliness
But whose houses
Are throne rooms of chaos.

Be careful of men
Who are never wrong
They bury their flaws
In the vesture of self-delusion.

Be careful of men
Who curse the land
That once blessed them
They are like the fountains of Marah
Which spring forth bitterness.

Marah: Exo 15:23

Run my Race.

I will run my race
I will stay on my lane
So as not to run in vain.

When I run,
Either on the muddy grass
Or on the hard floor
I run, yelling at myself
To be better than I was yesterday.

While I learn
The endurance and tenacity
That made you
The athlete the world adores
I will grind my knees
Until I reach my goal.

The roaring of cheering crowds
Or the absence of their applause
Means nothing to me
All I seem to hear
Is to finish my race.

I will run my race
I will finish my course
For it is vain
to sprint the path
I ought not to trek.

Scoffers

Keep scoffers far
As heaven and hell
Dig a deep pit
Impossible for them to cross
To the palace of your heart.

Keep scoffers far
As heaven and hell
Before the bridge of honour
You took years to build
Is laid to waste.

Keep scoffers far
As heaven and hell
Their path is full of chaos
And speech entrenched in disorderliness.

Keep scoffers far
As heaven and hell
Before you are consumed
With toxins
That exhume from their lips.

Hold Dearly

Hold dearly
Men who gave their all
To make you a better person.

Hold firmly
The words they spoke
Into the soil of your heart.

Learn Daily
To adore their strengths
And learn from their flaws.

Learn Daily
To watch your path
Lest you stray.

When Bars Are Raised

When the bars are raised
The Eagle comes out to the show
She flaps her wings
As she sets for flight
Gleefully, she glides above the bar
She was born for flight

When the bars are dropped,
The Ducks and Hens steal the show
They play hide and seek
On the lowered pole
The plain where they can only thrive

When the bars are raised,
Ingenuity becomes the norm.

Shut Off

Shut the door of your ears
To men who continually
Sing songs of your unworthiness
For anything good.

Close the gate of your heart
That their vicious venomous words
Will not cripple the courageous bones of your heart.

Rise daily
Above the hatred of men
Stand on the plateau
Where acrimony can barely thrive.

Virus of Hatred

Who will save our daughters
From this virus of hatred and bitterness
Directed towards their brothers?

Who will preserve their paths
From those who will poison their voices
To justify their intended evil?

Who will save our sons
From this malady of wealth at all cost
Where they sacrifice their sisters
On the shrine of greed and covetousness?

Who will open their eyes to see
Wealth gotten through blood
Will be lost through much blood?

Who will stop this selfish war
Between our sons and daughters
So that together they can fight
This evil of evils?

Silence

Silence wants to speak
But the world is not ready
To hear what he has to say
What will he say, they quirked?
Silence wants to speak,
But his words are too much
For the world to contain.

Silence,
Full of words unspoken
Waits for his voice to be heard
His voice hangs in the air
Like beautiful balloons
In an elite party
Yet no one hears
These noiseless sounds that fill the room.

Silence
Thought it was wisdom
To speak out against tyranny
He waited like a jilted bride
For a right time that will never come.

Silence walked into his grave with his breath
Holding insights that was never heard
Because he waited for the right time
That never came.

Rage.

I saw rage
Like the outburst of strong ocean waves
The quake that broke the spine of the sea
Made the sea to respond with fury
Forcefully roaring into the city
Like a wounded lion
Pulling down ageless structures
Wiping off a generation in a sweep.

I watched rage
Like the anger of a Diary Bull
Triggered by the prey
Who wants to feed on the young bull.
He locked his horns into the heart of the prey
Ripping out its lungs
Until breath became its visitor.

I can feel rage,
In the mouth of many
The pervasive words of hatred and bitterness
That can turn the day to night
Bring winter in summer
From those who have embraced pain as a norm
And blurred the line between love and hate.

I can see rage,
The kind history is wary of
Fueled by fear and distrust
And wrapped in the robe of selfishness.

Persevere

How would you feel
When you discover you backed down
When your hands have touched the knob
Of a great threshold?

What would you say
When you leave the mine
When just a little more hits
Would have opened the gold
Buried in the earth?

What would you do
When you discover
You've walked out of a room
Full of bread
Just to scavenge for crumbs like an orphaned dog?

What would you do
When you discover
You gave up easily to defeat
Without throwing a jab.

I will persevere
Until the opening of a great threshold
Until the unveiling of the goldmine
Until my jabs weaken defeat
I will persevere
Will You?

Hoho-Haha: The Song of the Birds

It was serenity with palpable calmness
The summer sun grinned widely at the sand dunes
The desert birds harmoniously hooted a melody
Hoho-haha Hoho-haha Hoho-haha
It's a good day to be alive.

Hoho-haha Hoho-haha Hoho-haha
The strong winds have
thrown the sands into the sky
With thoughts of ripping it apart
And leaving it homeless
The wind forgot the rage of the storm is momentary
The sands were laid to rest beautifully as dunes.

Hoho-haha Hoho-haha Hoho-haha
Let the winds blow, the birds sing
With the sands in the sky, not with anxiety
But with the excitement of a new home
Hoho-haha Hoho-haha Hoho-haha
The birds sing on the sand dunes

Epilogue

Don't Blame Me

I stood in front of the mirror
With a firm gaze at my image
I asked myself-
Who will I blame
if I don't turn out well?

My thoughts ran like wild air
Looking for who could shoulder
the blame, at least the burden of guilt
won't be mine to bear.

I paused,
at the seas of opportunities
that passes bye daily.
I paused,
at lovely moments
I had watched waste away.

The times I chose ease,
And I was satisfied with the momentary pleasure,
Rather than peruse the horrors of disciplined rigour
I succumbed to the fever of doubtful news.

I whispered at the mirror
until my voice exploded-
If I don't turn out well,
I have myself to blame.

If you don't turn out well,
Don't blame me.

ABOUT THE AUTHOR

Oyedolapo Oyesiji is a researcher, content writer and copywriter based in Canada. He loves writing, teaching, and reading. He has substantive experience in research, content writing, content strategy and development.

You can reachout to him via – oooyesiji@gmail.com or follow him on LinkedIn - @oyedolapooyesiji

GLOSSARY

YORUBA WORDS AND PHRASES USED IN THE TEXT

Abeje ------------------------------- a name for girls one who was begged for, usually from the gods

Adigun --- a name for boys which means the righteous

Adio --- a name for boys which means to be righteous

Aduke ----- a name for girls which means the one people fight for to pamper or take care of

Ajoke ---------- Ade a name for girls which means the one people jointly pamper or take care

Àkànbí ------ a name for boys which means the one that was consciously or deliberately given birth to

Akanji ----------------------------- a name for boys which means the one whose touch gives life

Amebo --- gossips

Amope -------------------- a name for girls which means the one whose knowledge is complete

Arike ------------------------------ a name for girls which means the one who is blessed on sight

Aroko --- a coded message

Eledua --- God

Farabalè -- calm down

Gbéra nle --- rise up or stand up

Ìbàdí àrán --- buttocks of velvet

Mi --- mine

Ojaoba --- the King's market

Okùnrin Ogun --- the man of war

Opeke --- a beautiful young girl

Oreke --- a beautiful lady

Orente --- a beautiful girl

Ti paa mi -- have killed me

fog, 2
folly, 15
fool, 77, 82
Forgiveness, iv, 12, 46
freedom, 37
Freelanced, 44
fresh rays of the sun, x
furnace, 106

G

gardener, 37
Gbéra nle, 47
globe, 6
God, iv, 9, 21, 22, 28, 29, 31, 35, 46
god that begs, 28
gods, 39, 60
Gold, 106
Good and Evil, 9
greed and materialism, 11
Guillotine, 87

H

haemorrhaging in pain., 8
Harbinger, 9
hare-brained, 79
harmony;, 55
hatred, 81
Healing, 13
hell, 7, 24, 31, 37, 93, 113
Hoho-haha, 121
Hold on, x
Holywood, x
honeycomb, 40
Hope, iv, 2, 9, 15, 16, 46, 92
hub of ingenuity, 69
Hurricane Maria, 5
husky-adults, 20
hustle for survival, 32
hypocrisy, 38

I

Ìbàdí àrán, 66

ice crystals, 33
immortality in mortality, 19
Iroko tree, 33
cyclones, 33

J

journey, 15

k

Keep scoffers far, 113
Khalesi, 40
King, 27
Kingdom, vi, 39, 40, 103

L

lava, 91
life imprisonment, 7
Light and darkness, 3
Light., iv, 14, 34
living dead, 16
Lord, 27
Love, 1, iv, v, 7, 9, 10, 34, 35, 41, 42,
43, 45, 46,
48, 50, 54, 56, 59, 65, 67, 95, 105
love-drought world, 6
lover, 42, 50

M

magma, 91
Marah, 111
Mount Everest, 97

N

New Man, 21
Nina Simeone's Blackbird, 83

0

ocean, 26, 94, 119
offence, 8, 81
okùnrin ogun, 47

www.ingramcontent.com/pod-product-compliance
Lightning Source LLC
Chambersburg PA
CBHW021124160726
47993CB00016B/2301